On the Wing

Contents

Claire Llewellyn

OXFORD

Who has wings?

Many animals have **wings**.
Their wings help them to fly.

owl

dragonfly

bat

hummingbird

ladybird

Flying helps animals to:
- find food
- get away from danger
- find a safe place to rest.

Dragonfly

A dragonfly has four wings. The wings are covered with **soft skin**. They help the dragonfly to move fast.

soft wings

The dragonfly finds food near water. Its wings help it to fly low and fast over the water. It catches insects and eats them.

Ladybird

A ladybird has two soft wings that it uses for flying. It also has two hard wing covers.

hard wing covers

soft wings for flying

The soft wings help the ladybird to fly away from danger. The hard wing covers **protect** the soft wings when the ladybird is not flying.

Bat

skin on wings

A bat has wings that are covered with skin. They help the bat to fly very fast.

A bat flies down to catch a moth.

Some bats eat insects. Their wings help them to catch the insects as they fly.

Owl

An owl has wings that are covered with soft **feathers**.

an owl's wing

feathers

Owls eat small animals like mice.

The owl flies low over the ground. It looks for food. Animals do not hear it as its feathers are so soft.

Hummingbird

wing feathers

A hummingbird has wings that are only 5cm long.

The hummingbird's wings move so fast you can hardly see them!

The hummingbird feeds from flowers as it flies. Its wings can move very fast. They help the hummingbird to stay in one place as it feeds.

Penguin

Not all animals with wings can fly. A penguin has wings but it can not fly.

wing

Penguins find food in the sea.
The penguin uses its wings to swim
fast. It dives down to catch fish.

Penguins also use their wings to
get away from danger in the sea.

Glossary

feather   light, soft parts that cover a bird

protect   to keep safe

skin   the covering of the body

soft   not hard. Cotton wool is soft.

wing   part of a bird, animal or insect, a bit like an arm